INTRODUCTION

Once in a while a young baseball player seems to step out of nowhere and perform as if he were a superman from another planet. Fernando Valenzuela did not come from another planet. He grew up playing baseball in a tiny Mexican town.

When he was still a teen-ager, he was discovered by a scout from the Los Angeles Dodgers. Speaking no English, Fernando bravely left his country and came to the United States. In his first season in the major leagues, with the help of his fantastic screwball, he became a living baseball legend.

SPORTS STAR

Fernando Valenzuela

S. H. BURCHARD

Illustrated with photographs

Harcourt Brace Jovanovich, Publishers
San Diego   New York   London

PHOTO CREDITS
Rob Brown (*Los Angeles Herald Examiner*):
pp. 2, 6, 27, 38, 42–43, 52, 62.
Wide World Photos: cover, pp. 9, 11,
13, 15, 16, 18–19, 22–23, 28.
Anne Knudsen (*Los Angeles Herald Examiner*):
pp. 24, 36–37.
United Press International: pp. 29,
44, 47, 49, 51, 55, 59, 61.
Steve Krauss (*San Antonio Express/News*): p. 33.

Requests for permission to make copies of any part of the work should be mailed to: Permissions, Harcourt Brace Jovanovich, Publishers, 757 Third Avenue, New York, New York 10017.

Printed in the United States of America

LIBRARY OF CONGRESS CATALOGING IN PUBLICATION DATA
Burchard, S. H.   Sports star, Fernando Valenzuela.
SUMMARY: A biography of the pitcher for the Los Angeles Dodgers who was the first rookie to win the Cy Young Award, the greatest honor a professional pitcher can earn.
1. Valenzuela, Fernando, 1960-   —Juvenile literature.
2. Baseball players—Mexico—Biography—Juvenile literature.
3. Los Angeles Dodgers (Baseball team)—Juvenile literature.
[1. Valenzuela, Fernando, 1960-
2. Baseball players]   I. Title.
GV865.V34B87 1982   796.357′092′4   [B]   [92]   82-47932
ISBN 0-15-278044-0   ISBN 0-15-278045-9 (pbk.)
B C D E   B C D E (pbk.)

CONTENTS

1

THE BOY FROM ETCHOHUAQUILA

The young man standing in front of a row of microphones and the TV cameras smiled shyly as he accepted one of baseball's highest honors, the 1981 Cy Young Award. "I feel very great being in the major leagues and winning the Cy Young Award in my first season," he said through an interpreter.

The Cy Young Award is given each year to two pitchers—one in the National League and one in the American—both voted the best in their leagues that season. It is the greatest honor that a professional pitcher can earn. Fernando Valenzuela was the first rookie ever to win the award. Just one week before he received it, Fernando had celebrated his twenty-first birthday.

To almost all sports fans, it seemed remarkable that such a young man could become one of baseball's best pitchers in only one year of professional play. It was not so surprising to Fernando. He had been working on mastering the game of baseball for most of his life.

Fernando was born November 1, 1960, in the tiny farming village of Etchohuaquila on the west coast of Mexico. He was the twelfth—and last—child of Avelino and Emergilda Valenzuela. He was also the seventh son.

When Fernando was born in this house (where his family still lives), there was no electricity and no television aerial.

The house where Fernando was born was made of whitewashed adobe with a roof of mud and sticks. Fernando and his brothers slept in the living room, some of them on a mattress that was used as a sofa during the day. Chairs pushed together made another bed. The rest of the family slept in the only bedroom in the house.

The land around Etchohuaquila is rocky, dry desert land. It is dotted with cactus plants. The Valenzuela family was very poor. They had half an acre of land in back of their house where they grew beans and corn. Mr. Valenzuela was proud to own his own land, but he did not earn enough money from his crops to support his large family. While Avelino worked on the family plot, the older Valenzuela boys helped bring in extra money by going to work in nearby fields owned by rich ranchers.

Despite being poor, Fernando had a happy childhood. He was very close to the members of his family, and he had many friends in the community where he lived.

When he was small, Fernando would sleep outside on warm nights. The hard ground was better than sleeping on a

Fernando's grade school
in Etchohuaquila

crowded mattress. Roosters would wake him up in the morning. Before it was light he could hear the sounds of trucks bumping along the dirt roads coming to pick up his older brothers and other villagers to take them to work in nearby fields. As a little boy, his work consisted of helping in the family garden, but he knew that one day he too would have to work in the fields with his brothers. He dreaded the idea.

Fernando and the other young boys in the village went to school. It was just a short

walk. Fernando was a good student, but on very nice days he and his friends would sometimes stop at an empty field to play baseball or soccer. His teachers told his parents that on some days Fernando played ball instead of going to school. His parents may have been unhappy that Fernando was missing his lessons, but they were probably too busy working to support their large family to worry too much about it. Fernando therefore may have learned to play baseball before he learned to read and write.

Another thing Fernando liked to do was to sit in a grove of fruit trees thinking and dreaming. He was a quiet and serious boy. His ancestors were Mayan Indians, who are remembered as being a serious people. Like many Mexican boys, Fernando may have had dreams of getting away from the life of a field worker by earning a living as a great athlete.

Most Mexican children play either soccer or baseball. Fernando played both, but he much preferred baseball. "God put the talent in my arm, not my feet," he once said.

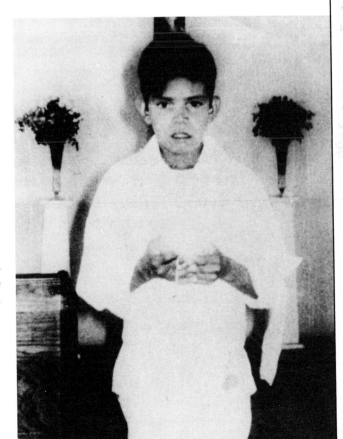

At nine years of age, Fernando makes his First Communion in the village Catholic church.

In small Mexican towns baseball games are big events. All of the Valenzuela boys liked to play baseball and were members of their home-town team. When Fernando was old enough to play on the town team, it was made up mostly of the Valenzuela brothers. Rafael pitched. Francisco played second, and Daniel played shortstop. Gerardo was the third baseman. Manuel was in the outfield, and Avelino pitched in relief. They thought Fernando was too young to pitch, so he was put on first base.

When he was about ten years old, Fernando began to collect stray balls and claimed they belonged to him. His friends called him Zurdo Robales, which means the "left-handed robber."

Fernando was shy, but when he was thirteen, he insisted that he be given a

Fernando's parents,
Avelino and Emergilda
Valenzuela

chance to pitch in a regulation game. He remembers the day well. He pitched two innings and struck out two batters. Then he was taken out because the coach thought he was too young to pitch.

2

LEAVING

HOME

As a young teen-ager, Fernando did not know very much about life outside of Etchohuaquila. When electricity came to the town in the early 1970s, he began to learn a little about the outside world by listening to the Mexican Pacific Coast League baseball games on the radio. He then started to think more seriously about becoming a professional ballplayer.

In May, 1976, when Fernando was fifteen years old, his home-town team went to play in a regional tournament held in Navojoa, a large town about twenty miles north of Etchohuaquila. Fernando pitched in the championship game. He lost, but some important Mexican baseball officials were there to watch him on the mound.

Team photo of players from Navojoa, Mexico. The arrow points to a slim Fernando.

Mr. Avelino Lucero, the manager of the Navojoa team, had to choose the best players in the Mexican state of Sonora to be on an all-star team. That team would play in a tournament against all-star teams from other states in Mexico. He liked Fernando's style and had watched him strike out sixteen batters in an earlier game.

Fernando was happy to be chosen for the team. He did not really expect to play and did not in the first tournament game. But in the second game, when the bases were loaded with no outs and the score was tied, Fernando was sent out to pitch.

He did not have a glove of his own. He quickly looked around for a lefthander's glove, but there wasn't one in sight. He grabbed a righthanded glove and ran out to the mound. The crowd booed the skinny kid who looked much too young to be pitching in a state tournament and did not even know what kind of glove to wear.

Fernando went right to work. He got three batters out without allowing a single run. The boos quickly changed to cheers.

A short time later Fernando played in another all-star tournament and was named the most valuable player in the tournament. When he went back home, he was offered a contract to play professional baseball for $250 for three months. Fernando agreed at once. He would never have to skip school again or go to work in the fields. At fifteen years of age, Fernando Valenzuela became a professional baseball player.

His mother was crying when the family came to see him off at the bus station. Fernando was near to tears himself as he said good-bye to his parents. He was afraid to leave his home, but he was also eager for his new career.

For the next few years, Fernando worked his way up in the Mexican leagues, playing for several different teams. It was not an easy life. Mexican professional ballplayers do not live as well as those in the United

States. Fernando spent most of his time on long bus rides, where sometimes he did not get a seat and had to sleep on the floor.

Also, the Mexican ball parks cannot be compared with those in the United States. At the ball park in Tampico, a port on the Gulf of Mexico, railroad tracks run across the outfield. Each time a train chugs across the field, the game has to be halted.

Still, for Fernando, it was an exciting way to live. He could play his favorite game all year around, and he was good at it.

Being a professional ballplayer did not change Fernando's personality. He was still quiet and shy. He was so quiet that some of his teammates said he spoke only in sign language. He nodded his head for "yes" and shook it for "no." He said "maybe" with a shake of his hands.

Valenzuela pitching
for the Navojoa Mayos

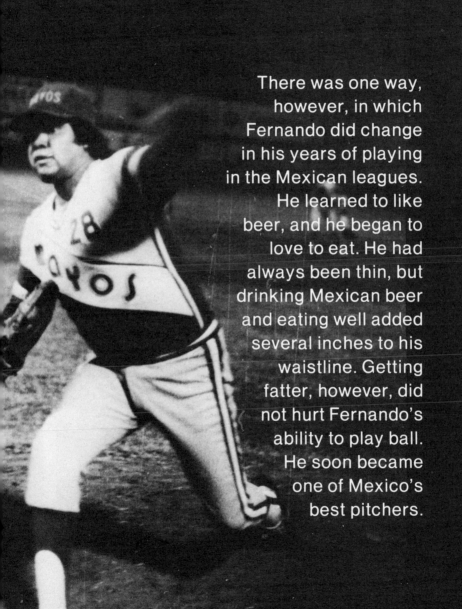

There was one way, however, in which Fernando did change in his years of playing in the Mexican leagues. He learned to like beer, and he began to love to eat. He had always been thin, but drinking Mexican beer and eating well added several inches to his waistline. Getting fatter, however, did not hurt Fernando's ability to play ball. He soon became one of Mexico's best pitchers.

3

THE
BIG BREAK

Mike Brito, who likes to wear fancy hats and smoke big cigars, is a scout for the Los Angeles Dodgers. He once played baseball for the Washington Senators, but in one game he wrecked his elbow in a collision at first base. For a while after that he played in the Mexican leagues. Finally he quit as a player and drove an RC Cola truck in Los Angeles. On the side he ran an amateur baseball league. On one of his teams was a pitcher named Bobby Castillo. Brito talked the Dodgers into hiring Castillo. Soon thereafter, Mike Brito became a full-time scout for the Dodgers.

One of Brito's first assignments was to go to Silao, Mexico, to look at a shortstop in a Mexican rookie league. He got there in the middle of March, 1978. It was Holy Week in Silao, and all the hotels were filled. Brito spent the night sleeping on the only four chairs in the local bus station.

He was stiff the next day when he went to the game to check out the shortstop. It was not an easy game to scout. There was no grass on either the infield or the outfield. Balls took bad bounces on the hard dirt.

After four innings Brito was disgusted. The shortstop was nothing special. Brito was afraid he had taken a long trip and

Mike Brito

spent a sleepless night for nothing. But then he began to watch the young pitcher on the opposing team. He was a lefty with a good fastball, and he was striking out a lot of batters. Brito moved behind home plate to get a better view. In one inning Fernando retired the side without a run after the bases had been loaded with no one out. Mike Brito began to get excited.

He could see that the pitcher had tremendous talent. After the game Brito talked to the team owner, who told him that Fernando was too young and to come back in a couple of years.

The following year the general manager of the Dodgers, Al Campanis, went to Mexico to watch Fernando, who was then pitching for a team in the state of Yucatan. He liked what he saw and began trying to buy Fernando from his Mexican team.

The family of Fernando Valenzuela. Fernando's mother, Emergilda, and his father, Avelino, are seated on the sofa behind the group of kneeling children.

Mike Brito made it his job to win over the Valenzuela family. He made daily trips over the dusty dirt roads to visit Fernando's family. Emergilda Valenzuela worried about her baby who didn't speak English and had never been out of Mexico. Mike Brito promised the Valenzuelas that he would take good care of their son.

On July 6, 1979, an agreement was reached. The Dodgers paid the Mexican team $120,000 for the eighteen-year-old pitcher. Fernando was sent to a minor league team in Lodi, California, for the rest of the season.

Fernando was lonely there. He missed his home, and he did not have any friends. He also missed his girl friend, Linda Margarita Burgos, who lived in Yucatan, Mexico. She was his first and only girl friend. But his loneliness did not affect his pitching arm. In twenty-four innings of play for the Lodi team, Fernando gave up three earned runs.

That winter Fernando played for the Instructional League in Arizona. Campanis sent Dodger pitcher Bobby Castillo to teach

Fernando how to throw one of the most difficult pitches in baseball—the screwball.

The screwball is a curve ball that breaks away from a righthanded hitter. It can also curve downward. It is very difficult to hit, but not very many pitchers use it. The reason they don't is that it is hard to control, and it puts a tremendous strain on a normal throwing arm.

It usually takes a pitcher several years to master the screwball. Fernando learned to throw it well in a couple of months and quickly became famous for the use he made of it.

On the baseball field Fernando was always happy. Off the field he was homesick and lonely. At spring training in Vero Beach, Florida, in 1980, his teammates began calling him Señor Silent. He didn't say much in Spanish, and he didn't talk at all in English.

After spring training Fernando was sent to play for a Dodger minor league team in San Antonio, Texas. Slowly he began to overcome his shyness, and he made some friends on the team. In addition, he liked San Antonio because there were many fans who spoke Spanish there. Soon he had a new nickname. "Señor Silent" became "The Chief."

The stands began to be packed every time the Mexican pitcher was on the mound. San Antonio fans grew to love Fernando and behaved as if he belonged to them.

Just as Fernando led San Antonio into the play-offs, the Los Angeles Dodgers sent for him. They were in a race for the pennant,

Fernando pitching
for San Antonio

and they desperately needed pitching help.

Fernando became a major-league pitcher in the final weeks of the 1980 baseball season after pitching in only thirty minor-league games. He was sorry to leave San Antonio, but he was also thrilled to have graduated to the major leagues. He liked, too, being able to fly on the Dodgers' private jet, being able to stay in first-class hotels, and being able to spend $29 a day on food!

Fernando did not disappoint the Dodgers. He played with the steadiness and the calmness of an experienced professional. In the ten times he came in as a relief pitcher, which covered a total of seventeen and two-thirds innings, Fernando allowed no runs. He struck out sixteen batters.

His first win came in a game against the

Giants on September 30. His second came in the opener of the final series with the Astros, who were three games ahead of the Dodgers in the pennant race. The Dodgers went on to win the last two games of the season but lost the pennant in the play-off game. Fernando did his best to save the game when he pitched two innings of shutout relief. Manager Tommy Lasorda may have wished he had started his rookie pitcher.

Fernando had no regrets. He had made it to the major leagues in the United States at the age of nineteen. In the short time he spent with Los Angeles at the end of the 1980 season, he had captured the heart of the Mexican community that surrounded Dodger Stadium.

Fernando giving
a pitching demonstration
at Little League day
in east Los Angeles

4

FERNANDO FEVER

When the Los Angeles Dodgers opened their 1981 season, they had no idea that a new disease was about to strike the city and later the whole country. It would be called Fernando Fever.

On the opening day of the new baseball season, the Dodgers faced the Houston Astros. Four of the starting Dodger pitchers were hurt or sick. Manager Tommy Lasorda had very little choice. He decided to start

Fernando, who had been promoted to a starter during spring training.

The fans knew Fernando had done well as a relief pitcher at the end of the 1980 season, but they were not sure he was ready to pitch in a game as important as the opening one. Fernando did not seem worried. After batting practice, he lay down to rest on a trainer's table and went to sleep.

When the game got under way, Fernando marched out proudly to the pitcher's mound with his back straight. There were no cheers from the fans. Fernando's first pitch was a screwball on the outside corner of the plate. Astro batter Terry Puhl swung and missed. The fans clapped their approval.

As the innings rolled by, Fernando had almost perfect control of the ball and never showed any sign of being nervous. The fans began to sense that they were watching someone and something special.

When Fernando threw the last strike in the ninth inning, he was the winning pitcher. The Dodgers won 2-0. Fernando had pitched a five-hit shutout.

Dodger catcher Mike Scioscia ran out to hug his pitcher. Each one of the Dodger players shook Fernando's hand. The crowd stood and chanted, "Fernando, Fernando," over and over again. It was the beginning of Fernando Fever.

After the opening game the Dodgers went on the road. On the trip Fernando pitched two more shutouts and one game in which he allowed only one run.

Fernando Fever rapidly spread to the rest of the country. A new cheer could be heard at each of the big-league ball parks.

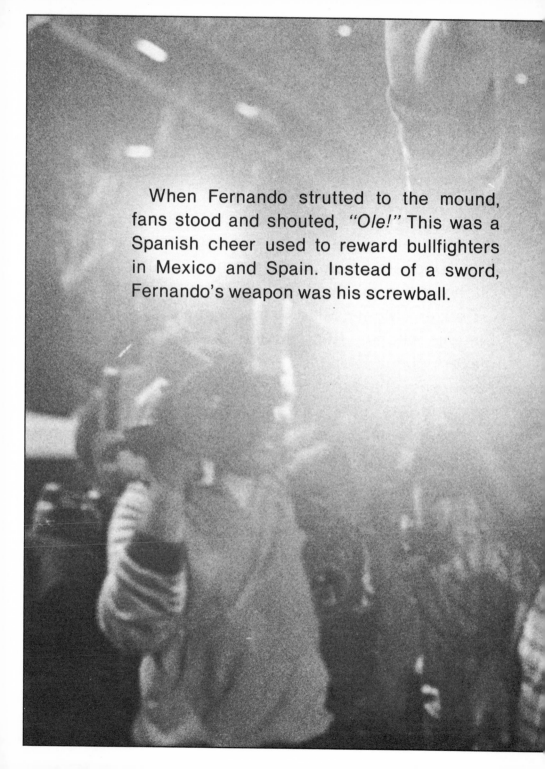

When Fernando strutted to the mound, fans stood and shouted, *"Ole!"* This was a Spanish cheer used to reward bullfighters in Mexico and Spain. Instead of a sword, Fernando's weapon was his screwball.

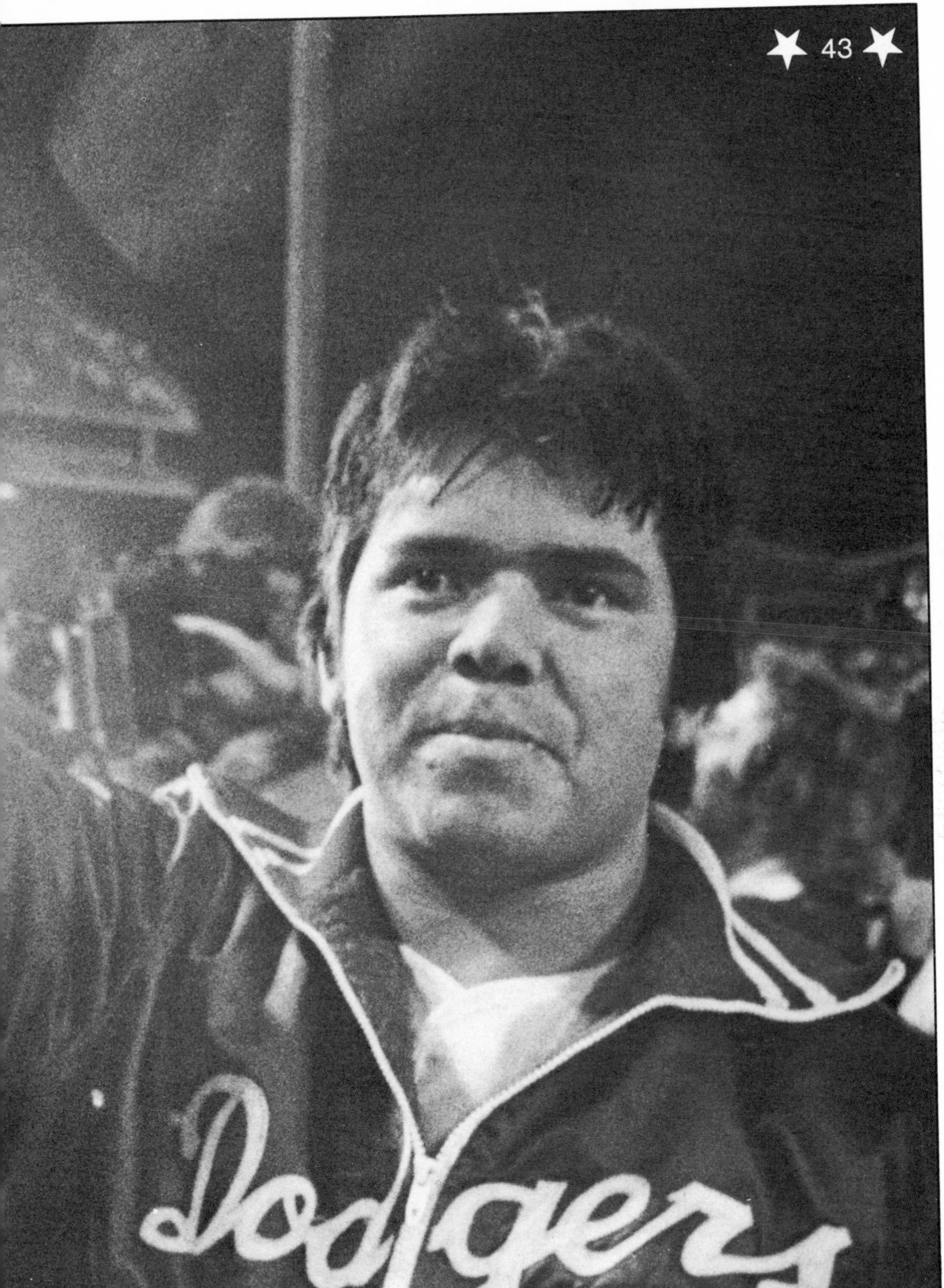
Dodgers

When Fernando returned to Los Angeles after the road trip, he was the National League leader in wins, strikeouts, earned run average, and shutouts. All the tickets to his homecoming game against the San Francisco Giants had been sold for a week.

Fernando was not at his best that night, but his team helped him to a 5–0 victory. When he singled in his first time at bat, the big crowd gave him a standing ovation. Fernando was told to tip his hat to his enthusiastic fans.

In addition to being a great pitcher, he was a good hitter and an excellent fielder. The only thing Fernando did not do well was run. He was too heavy to be fast.

Fernando kept on winning. He had eight straight victories. Deafening cheers began to greet him each time he took the mound.

Fernando is congratulated by a teammate after a victory. Number 14 is the Dodger catcher, Mike Scioscia.

Fernando was living in a motel in the Mexican section of Los Angeles near the stadium. Crowds of fans began gathering there to get a look at their hero. Fernando was often too timid to go out and face them. When he was not at the ball park or traveling, he spent most of his time alone inside his motel room watching television. He became a television addict. His favorite programs were the cartoons, especially the Pink Panther. He also enjoyed watching soap operas. It was from television that he began to learn English.

Fernando planned to marry his girl friend from Mexico and bring her to share his life in the United States, but he wanted to wait until he was firmly settled in this country.

Mike Brito began to worry that the young pitcher spent too much time alone. He

Fernando surrounded by reporters
at a press conference

remembered his promise to Emergilda Valenzuela. He therefore invited Fernando to live with him. The young pitcher was happy to move in with the Britos, but he did not give up his passion for television or for drinking beer and eating—particularly New York strip steak, pizza, and tortillas.

So many reporters wanted to interview him that for the first time in Dodger history

Manager Lasorda had to organize full-scale press conferences in which his shy pitcher, who still spoke very little English, could meet with a hundred or more reporters at one time. An interpreter translated the questions into Spanish for Fernando and turned his answers into English for the reporters. Fernando often conducted the interviews with his aching pitching arm submerged in a tub of ice.

After he had put together an incredible eight-game winning streak, the Dodgers flew Fernando's parents and his sister Dolores to watch a Valenzuela game. It was their first trip away from home and the first time they had ever seen Fernando pitch professionally. Surrounded by 52,437 other fans in Dodger Stadium, they watched him lose to the Philadelphia Phillies, 4–0. That

Fernando's father, Avelino, watches while his son shows a group of fans how to hold the ball for a screwball pitch.

was the first time anybody had seen him lose in the big leagues.

Fernando was not too upset. He knew he had to lose sometimes. When asked about how they felt about their son's success, his parents gave the quiet reply, "We are proud of what he does. He is a good boy."

As the season wore on, Fernando began to relax more with his teammates. He

learned enough English to tell a few jokes, and he made some friends. He also taught his teammates a little Spanish. Fernando often chewed bubble gum while he was sitting in the dugout. Tommy Lasorda and others teased him by trying to pop his giant bubbles.

At his invitation, Linda came up to visit him. Fernando was proud to show her around his new country.

There have been other rookie pitchers who have shown great promise at the start of a season, but none has ever been able to pitch as well for an entire season as Fernando. The year 1981, however, was the season that was interrupted by a long strike between the ballplayers and the owners. As a result, there were fewer games played than in normal years.

Fernando's fiancée,
Linda Burgos

At the end of the two 1981 seasons (the one before and the one after the strike), it was Fernando Valenzuela who led the National League in four pitching categories. He had pitched eleven complete games. He had eight shutouts—a league record for a rookie. He had pitched 192 innings and had 180 strikeouts.

It had been quite a year. When there was so much talk about money and strikes, it was good for the country to have an amazing young pitcher like Fernando Valenzuela enter the game.

5

THE 1981 PLAY-OFFS, THE WORLD SERIES, AND A WEDDING

With a lot of help from Fernando, the Dodgers won the National League West title for the first half of the split season. The Houston Astros won the title for the second half—the part after the strike ended.

The Dodgers then met the Astros in a mini series to determine the National League West champion. The first team to win three games would be the winner.

The Dodgers lost the first two games, but they did not give up. With Burt Hooton pitching, they won the third game. When Fernando pitched and won the fourth game to tie the series, there was such a big celebration in Los Angeles that the noise could be heard for miles around. The fifth game would decide the National League West title, and the Dodgers won it by a score of 4–0, becoming the first team in baseball history to win a five-game play-off series after trailing by two games.

The team had very little time to get ready to meet the Montreal Expos for the National League championship. On a warm fall day just two days after beating Houston, Burt Hooton took the mound for the Dodgers and won the first game by a score of 5–1.

Fernando Valenzuela was to pitch in the

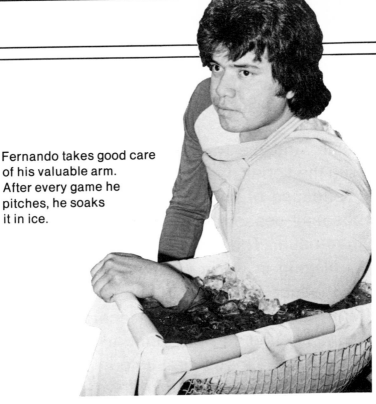

Fernando takes good care of his valuable arm. After every game he pitches, he soaks it in ice.

second game. He would be working with only three days' rest.

"He's done it before," said Manager Tommy Lasorda. "Seven times in fact. He'll have all winter to rest."

Fernando and the Dodgers were not able to beat the Expos. They lost the second game, and the two teams flew to Montreal with the series tied at one game apiece.

Because of the baseball strike, the 1981 baseball season had ended later in the fall than usual. The Dodgers were a team used to playing in warm weather. They not only had to face the cold mid-October weather in Montreal, but they had to face a Canadian team fighting for the right to play in the World Series for the first time.

When the game in Montreal began, the temperature was 46 degrees F (8 degrees C). The Dodgers lost by a score of 4–0.

Once more the Dodgers were behind. They had to win two games in a row to win the National League championship. They won the first one with Burt Hooton pitching. The series was tied at two games apiece.

Fernando was scheduled to pitch in the

fifth and deciding game of the series. Shortly after the first ball was thrown out on Sunday, October 18, it began to rain. After three and a half hours of icy rain had fallen, the game was finally canceled.

When Fernando took the mound the next day, the temperature was 41 degrees F (5 degrees C). The artificial turf was crusty with ice. The pennant was to be decided under wintry conditions.

As it all turned out, it was decided in story-book style. Expo pitcher Ray Burris pitched eight tough innings of five-hit ball. Valenzuela pitched eight and two-thirds innings of three-hit ball. In the top of the ninth the two teams were tied, 1–1.

The Montreal star relief pitcher Steve Rogers was called in to pitch the ninth inning. With two outs, thirty-five-year-old

Rick Monday, who had been a major league player for fifteen years, hit a home run to win the game and the series for the Dodgers.

Again, there was no time to rest. The Dodgers raced to New York to face the New York Yankees in the World Series.

Once more, the Dodgers fell behind. They lost the first two games. The third game was played in Dodger Stadium with two star rookies doing the pitching. The Yankees' twenty-two-year-old pitching sensation, Dave Righetti, met the Dodgers' twenty-year-old hero, Fernando Valenzuela.

It was not a good night for either of the young pitchers. Righetti lasted for only a little over two innings. Fernando wasn't much better. When the Dodgers jumped out to a three-run lead in the first inning, he gave up four runs in the next two innings.

Tommy Lasorda decided to stick with his
young pitcher. He took out his starting
catcher, Steve Yeager, and replaced him
with Mike Scioscia. Yeager had caught
Valenzuela for a full game only twice during
the season. He sensed that the young
pitcher was uncomfortable with him. Mike
Scioscia and Fernando had learned to work
well together. Scioscia had even learned to

speak a little Spanish in order to confer with Fernando. Valenzuela began to settle down. He was often in trouble, but he didn't allow another run after the third inning. The Yankees changed pitchers several times.

Lasorda had faith in Fernando, who stuck it out and won. After the game Lasorda said, "Fernando was like a sharp poker player who had to bluff his way through."

Dodger Manager Tom Lasorda hugs his winning pitcher after capturing the National League championship.

The tide, with Fernando's help, had at last turned for the Dodgers. It had been a long, tough fight for the pennant, and they were determined to win it all. The Los Angeles Dodgers won the next three games and became the 1981 World Champions.

It was the kind of success story that usually happens only in fairy tales. Fernando had begun his rookie year with the Dodgers with eight victories in a row and ended the season with a World Series victory. His triumph was complete when he won the Cy Young Award and was voted the National League's Rookie of the Year. To top it all off, Fernando ended this fabulous year by going back to Mexico and marrying Linda, who had become a school teacher.

Fernando was even more of a hero in his own country of Mexico than in the United

States. Accounts of his victories usually appeared on the front pages of Mexican newspapers. In small towns where there were no newspapers, radios, or television sets, the people gathered in dusty town squares to listen to Fernando's games, which were broadcast over loudspeakers.

At the wedding ceremony Fernando looked very handsome in a black tuxedo. Linda wore a lacy $3,000 gown. Fernando

had to sneak into the church by a side door because the crowd of well-wishers was so huge. Two bishops and an archbishop presided at the ceremony. The wedding was broadcast to the Mexican nation.

After spending their honeymoon in Hawaii, Fernando and his new bride went back to the little village of Etchohuaquila. Fernando planned to spend the winter playing off-season ball for his old club, the Mayos. It was good to be back home, where he could relax surrounded by his family and friends.

In one season of playing ball in the United States the quiet, shy twenty-year-old had brought great color and excitement to professional baseball. And for Fernando Valenzuela, the 1981 season was just a beginning.

PITCHING RECORD

FERNANDO VALENZUELA

YEAR	CLUB	GAMES	INNINGS PITCHED	WINS	LOSSES	STRIKE-OUTS	BASES ON BALLS	GAMES STARTED	GAMES COMPLETED	SHUT-OUTS	EARNED RUN AVERAGE
1978	Guanajuato	16	93	5	6	91	46	13	6	0	2.23
1979	Yucatan	26	181	10	12	141	70	26	12	2	2.49
1979	Lodi	3	24	1	2	18	3	3	0	0	1.13
1980	San Antonio	27	174	13	9	162	70	25	11	4	3.10
1980	Dodgers	10	18	2	0	16	5	0	0	0	0.00
1981	Dodgers	25	192	13	7	180	61	25	11	8	2.48
MAJOR LEAGUE TOTALS		35	210	15	7	196	66	25	11	8	